AEGEAN
ARCHIVES

AEGEAN ARCHIVES

Poetry
by
George N. Argyros

DORRANCE & COMPANY • *Ardmore, Pennsylvania*

To Greece — the beloved land of my birth,
and to Barbara — my lover, wife, and companion.

Oh, destitute mortal!
Do not fret and tremble
like a delicate blossom
sensing the oncoming, lethal
wintry blast.
For there is only one
instant's breath
which separates your
temporal life
from that of permanence
amid the boundless
acres of the
asphodel fields.

SEA, MY SEA

Thalatta, my Thalatta,
when I see the calmness
of your supine countenance
I wonder, is it the reflection
of your depths,
or the tragedian's mask
that you wear
to hide your constant
turmoil?
And what of your bitter brine?
Your tears?
And your foamy waves?
The crown of your madness?

I saw a partridge on the wing,
another on its nest,
and I perceived creation,
this life, at its best.
I saw a rabbit on the run
inside an orchard green,
and with the youthful eyes of mine
the being that I've been.
And then a hunter shot and killed
the bird, the hare, and my dream
where in their blood I saw that life
is a perverted scheme
of some unknown power
and its satanic whim.

Better one moment's liberty
to breathe sweet freedom's air
than centuries of slavery
and tyranny's despair.

Pericles, arise from your eternal slumber
and deliver another famous
funeral oration;
not for our dead,
but for those of us who live.
Our ethical ramparts have
crumbled into dust,
and our crimes toward
ourselves and society,
like vipers who attack their
own flesh and die from
the self-inflicted wounds,
decimate our existence.

Let me bestow upon thy lips
the kiss of love,
and by the conflagration
which will follow,
observe the portals of eternity
swinging wide
to receive us.

Watching the flight
of my youthful dreams,
I see the invisible hand
of destiny
clip their wings,
and they crash upon
the rocky pinnacle
of my imagination
as another bitter tear
marks their grave.

Did you ever hear a soul crying?
Well, I did—
mine.
And unable to assist it, I cried;
for the rest of the world
became suddenly
deaf.

AN OLD MAN'S WISH

Ah, youth!
Why do you desert me so soon?
Ah, poor me!
If only you could retard your advance
and spare the wrinkles from my face.
I would exchange all my wealth
for love's beautiful grace.
Oh, youth!
Come once again
and brighten my old age.

MASTER PHIDIAS

Had I your kind of skill,
your mallet and your chisel,
I would sculpt
the most horrendous
beast of them all—
the human soul.
And then no more.
For its consummate ugliness,
would force mankind to mold
the counterpart of my work—
the beauty of his soul.

Like the furious fists
of a blinding blizzard,
love pounds my
quivering, heathen heart.

Amid the arctic solitude,
under the northern lights,
I hear the voice of loneliness
and like a child, I cry.
The crystallized brightness
of all the living stars
like a potent, sweet nepenthe
benumbs my aching heart.

Condemned to die by the chosen ones
of their society,
in the slaughterhouses
of foreign lands,
they fought valiantly and died.
But the cries of their undefiled death
will live forever
to pursue their chosen executioners.

BETRAYAL

The catafalques
have reached their destination,
and now all is quiet
except for the moaning of the dead
in the pantheon of the long-buried
fallen heroes.
They mourn for those who have just joined them,
who fought in vain,
and were betrayed.

Suppressed by the anthropomorphic mutants,
the should-be-great souls of the masses
pass on through the
earthly, transitory state—
obscured.

To be a dreamer is not a crime
if to reality what I conceived
I now bring without shame,
knowing none has been deceived.

A regal, towering mountain peak
pierced the white, soft clouds
and through the aperture I saw
seas of immortal crowds.
I heard the talk of ancient men
saw smiles of brave, young lovers—
all who I thought were dead;
and said,
"Hail, my eternal brothers."

Furiously, we race across the temples
of our childhood
where with sadistic haste
we bury the jewel of our existence,
our innocence,
only to return staggering,
godless, begging—
begging for the repossession
of what we so foolishly entombed.
But mute and desolate now
we stare into nothingness
while the echoes of our youth
reverberate in vain;
for we are all cursed
with age,
and are deaf.

A ray of the golden dawn,
a bird on the wing,
a flower in bloom
soothe my long-suffering soul;
and like a miracle they disperse
this dreary, mortal gloom.

As the thin, eerie mists of doubt
press heavily upon his aching heart,
with hope of succor
he raises his glance,
only to see his love
disappear
like the smoke of a burnt offering
into the blue of the evening,
leaving behind
in a pool of lingering,
aromatic memories, his existence,
crushed!

Footprints of the times
upon the dust of the ages
are quickly obliterated
by blissful but insidious,
creeping forgetfulness.

Rose petals in the wind
drift in the evening breeze,
and I, alone, like a dried
thorny stem
await the chill of the winter
while hoping
for a miracle.

Somewhere
upon the vast realms
of this universe
there is a candle of hope
for everyone.
But where is mine?
The darkness is unbearable
and hidden is the sky.

The latent flames of our souls
need but a brain's spark
to set ablaze creation's
forbidden, secret walls.

HOLLOW VICTORY

Countless white crosses that mark the silent graves,
the legless peddlers on the curbs,
the blinded tapping the sidewalk
with their steel-pointed canes,
and those deformed in their flesh and soul
by the war's hungry flames,
are the illustrious braves
who fought slavery's misery
only to become the thralls
of this premeditated, hollow victory.

I sought refuge in your ornate temples
and I found none.
I sought from you the answer to my pressing problems
and you gave me none.
I besought you to give me guidance
and you denied it to me.
I knelt and prayed and cried like a child,
for my children,
and you mocked at me.
I stood before your altar like one who is vanquished,
and you sneered at me.
Then suddenly I saw
that you were not there
where a god should be.
For you are nothing
but an alien, nonexistent being
which my ignorance and fear
had created to cover up the
incomprehensibility of the universe.
And I dried my eyes,
and I stood erect,
and I turned my face away from your altar,
and I walked away from your temple
to discover that what I sought from you
could only be found in the chambers of my soul,
and I bade you farewell,
oh, master of nothingness!

Yes, you shall come
    one Sunday afternoon.
And you shall lie
    on the April grass
to watch the miracle
    of a rosebush in bloom.
And you shall marvel
    at its sight, and pause
as I shall cut the first
    dew-sprinkled rose
to offer to you.
    For the moment that
I have waited for
    shall be that moment
when I'll cut the rose.
    And accept it, my sweet, you shall,
and your lips shall tremble
    like the stars.
And that present time shall revert
    to the distant past which was blessed
when I met you in my dreams,
    my love.

THE WONDER OF THE WANDERER

The tatters of a once-proud wanderer
bobbing on the dark seas, are the only remains
of the aftermath of his life's storm.
Yet the finger of fate still points
at that direction as if doubting his destruction.
But why?
Only the wanderer can answer this query.
Seek him not, for his secret will be revealed
to none but to the one who shall come
to stay, and who shall believe in the
wonder of the wanderer.

I stand alone
with only eternity
inside of me —
my soul.

Oh, how I wish
    that I were a beast
to live in ignorance,
    in utter bliss,
instead of being
    a human fool,
alive but betrayed
    by a kiss.

I wonder if
what we call life
is not death,
and death is life.
For I have tasted
the contents of life's chalice,
and they are bitter.
But what of death's?

Like a godless wanderer
starved and thirsty,
who quivers in the excruciating grip
of the blood-dripping, sharp talons
of a nightmare
that arises out of nowhere,
and has no beginning and no end;
I see myself helplessly
struggling
lest you vanish into nothingness
like the mists of Hades
that melt away and disappear
in the valleys of its chasms.

Prophets who spring up
from the deserts of hot sands
raise their ignorant voices
and create our monstrous gods.

Oh, my soul!
Lift up my sinking spirits.
Do not let me perish
in the battlefield
of my incoherent despair.
Let not the sabers of misery
destroy my existence.
Arrest the steel-booted, black despair which
tramples my diminishing faith.
Brace my quivering mind
with the shaft of hope
and breathe a whisper of courage
into the emptiness of my heart.
Tread down the horrendous
apparition of failure,
and spread your undefiled
aegis
to prevent the flaming arrows of defeat
from scorching my being
beyond recognition.
My soul, do not seal my destiny
with that of a vanquished caitiff,
but crown my lowered head
with a victor's laurels,
even if it is destined
that at the end
I should fall
and cease to be.

By ascending
the spires
of my dreams
that I hold,
I escape
the fires
of this blatant world.

THINKING OF NOVEMBER

In the garden
the dust of death
has fallen
upon my last
rosebud.
The owl has screeched;
the wind is blowing cold.
My offerings to you
are naught.
There are no roses
anymore.
And May is far,
far away.
What shall I do?
Nature has turned all grey
and my hands are empty of gifts for you.
Hold them until the buds return
lest they become limp
seeking to reach their own dust.

No god, no saint, no priest, no pope
has powers to forgive
that which a mortal's living soul
cannot or will not forgive.
For catharsis can be obtained
not from the outside domain
but from within one's hidden world
which is none other than the soul.

My soul and I
had a chat
in absolute seclusion,
and we agreed
that life is but
a maniacal confusion.

Oh, how I envy the imposing
towering rocks
that are carved by the sea,
and their brutal beauty
which the waves bathe
endlessly.
What overpowering
ecstasy inspires
their mute stillness
under the lightning and thunder
and the roaring of the foamy,
raging sea?
Only a seabird can tell,
resting amidst their
jagged peaks.

I tossed a coin and I wished
life's process to reverse.
And to my great amazement,
death preceded birth.
I joyed in lofty exultation
now that birth came after,
and raised my head defiantly,
and mocked my alien master.

I am envious
of the effortless and mute
accomplishment
of the mountains
that reach as far as I can see;
while I struggle
to avoid my fall
into the dank and blood-chilling
caverns of my
unknown tomorrow.

If I could only find my way back
far from life's ever-changing shores,
to the dreamland of my childhood,
when the snow was for play
and the tempest meant warmth,
and the nights were for dreaming
gentle dreams of tender love;
my tired eyes I would close
and leave the present for yore
and live there forevermore.

Wisdom is
the fulcrum
by which
we will move creation.

ICARUS

He soared.
He fell.
Agony succeeded
Ecstasy.
But from his
cup of death
up-sprung his
immortality.

As each god of ours
cruelly by us is tumbled,
our conscience is crumbled.
And while our ashes
ultimately will
contaminate our ancestral
burial grounds,
our souls will hover endlessly
above the infernal pyres
as their punishment—
for they owed their allegiance
to neither
paganism
        nor
monotheism,
but to their
body and soul's consuming master,
sadism.

In millions of burning, falling sparks
our life's flame is spent,
until in the twilight of our reign,
by death our knee is bent.

Come, my soul.
You and I, and you, my shadow,
we must hope, there's still tomorrow.
Lonesome though we are, all three,
we must fight to stay free.
Come, my soul, and you, my shadow,
follow me until tomorrow.
Who can tell what will be?
Life for all?
Or death for two
by despair's unerring arrow?
Come, my partners,
let us see!

Carved
by the dull and rusty
jagged-edged swords
of the unknown
tomorrow,
I stand alone
bleeding—
like a helpless,
innocent lamb
whose headless body
is ravished
by the sacrificial pyres
before the altar
of a bloodthirsty god.

In risky times our eyes behold
the workings of our brains.
But whence they come, these golden thoughts
to soothe our human pains?
Oh, in the morning perceive
the golden, new sunrise,
and in the evening see the stars—
how silently they rise;
and you will feel that pain cannot stand
such a divine surprise.

I envy the sea
and her brutal force—
for she can carve
her own limits
and I cannot.

When we were young
we could see ghosts,
but now that we are older,
we see the shadows
of those ghosts
merging with the nebulous
disillusion
of our impending dissolution.

THE SENTINELS OF THE UNIVERSE

Golden pinheads
upon the blue,
concave cushion –
glowing remote candles –
the silent, scintillating
sentinels of the universe –
in their unerring
nocturnal space litany.
The stars.

White sea curls
on the lips
of a cave,
briney blisters
on the shifting
sand,
the retreating look
of a stranded crab
from the forward aim
of a screaming
sea gull. . .

The moon was nothing
but an orbital slave
in the vast expanses of space,
until we looked at it
together.

You are the mountain;
I am the sea —
the unpredictable
versus
stability.
Yet none from the other
can be set free —
neither the mountain
nor the blue sea.
Such a sundering,
my love, would be
a most disastrous
calamity.

To express my inner feelings
I should have the seas for ink,
and for paper heaven's ceiling,
plus eternities to think.

On the anvil of
circumstance
and by the hammer of fate,
I am beaten to an insensate,
amorphous mass
until my sinews,
pulverized and dried,
dissipate into nothingness—
freeing the soul.

I'd rather be an anachronism
than drown
in this modern cataclysm.

Our blood is the ink,
our flesh the inkwell,
into which the bony hand of fate
dips its adamantine pen—
and on the pages of time
writes the history of man.

THE ONENESS OF GOD AND MAN

A leaping, serpentine flame
shatters the air and roars.
The faithful cower.
The heathen exalts.
Could it be Zeus,
the Thunderer himself,
who sends this fiery message
to my anachronistic heart?
Pray tell me,
for I am a pagan
and Zeus is in my heart
with all his loves,
his hate, his wrath.
I am the one whom you
can see.
He is the one whom you
cannot see.
We are both one—
I, the mortal,
and Zeus, my
burning alter ego.

Using some dirt for matter
the old
barbaric gods
fashioned in
crudest manner
us mortals,
as we are!

When I hear
the irresistible call
which will lead me through
the labyrinthine hall
to where mute stands,
magnificently bold,
the undisputed spark of the
forbidden world,
the inner sanctum
of the eternal soul—
I shall go in. To find, to probe.
And then, I shall depart
as I have entered in,
proud and bold and puzzled
but utterly exalted—
for I have gone
where none has ever gone,
and I have seen
what none has ever seen before—
the eternal citadel of hope
for afterlife—
the soul.

Unrelated patterns
edged in a mourning hue
twirl around the lanterns
of the distant blue.
Patterns in confusion
scattered by the winds
twirl in cold, dark space;
dreams without wings
form a past and future
which would never be
if I were a human
destined to be free.

Momentous
golden threads of rejoicings
interwoven
into the harsh fibers of time
render our life bearable.
Until the rhythm of our shuttle
is choked
by the hawsers of life
and falls limp
upon the broad nets
of time past.

THE QUICK AND THE DEAD

O river Styx
with your shrouded shores—
O enigmatic, liquid sphinx—
what angry god has made you thus?
Was it his blessing
or his curse
that free and bound souls alike
would stare across your banks
and lose their might?
Was he afraid of a combine
that would castrate
the divine?

I am
a wandering
infant of flesh,
subservient
to a breath,
a toddler,
captive
to the might
of the silent
sermon of death.

Only in the peak of the night
I possess what is not mine,
the legend of the past:
the glory of the fallen monarchs,
the sunken ruins of the ages,
and the footsteps
of the ancient
and vanished ranks
which have trod
the pathways of time.

Death is only metamorphosis.
I shall not fear
his coming.

Roses under a moon-flooded sky,
an audience of budding debutants,
slowly, secretly drop their
laced green scarfs
and blush
with every lusty note
of the nocturnal soloist —
the mockingbird.
Until dawn comes
with diamonds
in wee dewdrops
to stud their petal faces
and their hymenal burst.

I have seen
my bride
in the realms of her dreams,
a contented child
with a joyous smile.
And I tiptoed
out of her dreams
to kiss her lips
good night.

TO MY WIFE

Borne on a silent,
unfurled breath,
the unspoken words
of my inner self advance,
and order my laggard tongue
to give them sound
and sing a song.
But all my tardy
tongue can do
is to utter softly
"I love you."

I am
the ashes of my
forebears,
recycled
in that vast
chemical complex —
the womb.

The mist of an irate sea
swallowed the granite crags.
A shipwrecked mariner is sprawled
on a thin ribbon of beach,
far, far away from the din of life—
at rest at last.
A host of hermit crabs
sent by the foaming sea
circle his tattered corpse.
Could those be the souls
of his bereaved?

We leap
into the ballet
of life,
only to fall limp
on the lap
of death.

I am lashed
with the whip
of ecstasy
to an
agonizing
frenzy,
that ends
with the
sputtering
of my manhood
into the
sheathing folds
of your womb.

I am an
increment
of time's rule:
    multiplied,
    divided,
    subtracted. . .
and suddenly
    discarded,
    erased.

Before age
usurps our youth,
before the twilight
devours the dawn,
before the stars
wake the sun,
let us love!
Let the world spin on
as it pleases.
Come!

A NEW ROSEBUD

Soft puffs of mist
embrace the red rose.
Its exquisiteness
ensnared in their
temporal transparency
with the onrushing dawn.
A clear dewdrop
crowns its red-hued heart
to reign today with brilliance
to rival and surpass
the rising sun.

Loneliness is
a steel-toothed termite
which saps you within
and gnaws you without—
leaving only your bones
in a perforated shroud.

Plastic faces
behind the windshields,
hypnotized
by the thumping
rubber wheels,
staring at death
as they accelerate.

Adventures
in the realm of dreams.
Leaping thoughts with broken bridles
galloping through
the boulevards of sleep.
Exhausted, they cease
upon a memorial
to their vain struggle —
my crumpled pillow.

PYROTECHNICS

A comet is
the excrement
of time and space,
in a brilliant
and dramatic
presentation
for the earthlings,
by the renowned
designer
and producer—
the universe.

I, the man:
forged
between the anvil
of ignorance
and the hammer
of wisdom,
dipped
in the cauldrons
of liquified, alien spirits
to be tempered
for absolute freedom,
owing my
allegiance to none
save my soul.

I feel the touch
of spring's sensual fingers.
Their transcendental
magnetism transforms me
to a volcano.
I quiver helplessly.
I explode.
My molten lust
begins to spill
within and without.
I am seared
in my own passion,
the arsonist
that I am!

Oh, my angry, furious sea,
why do you swallow your own waves?
Is it because of your hungry wrath
for failing to tame your waters,
or to build your brutal force
for more mountainous waves,
which ultimately will bury us
inside your wet, dark graves?

Oh, sea, poor sea!
Why do you throw yourself
with such maddening force
upon the jagged granite rocks?
Is it revenge that you are seeking?
Oh, if you could only speak
instead of foaming.

IS THIS WHAT LIFE HAS TO OFFER?

Part I

Is this what life has to offer?
Is this what life has to give?
A thorny cradle without a cover,
a stolid, shrouded, emberless hearth?

My head I bow in utter shame
when I perceive what I did
to you, my impaired love, my hapless bride,
when your poor mind became diseased.

Possessed by bestial and cruel hate,
without a seed of noble faith,
I threw you into this serpent's cave
where even the dead dread life's stench,
and where the clenched fists of starving fates
beat hard upon your mind's fiends.

Is this what destiny had to offer,
and what the gods on you wished?
To rot in darkness like a pauper
without the ministrations of a priest
or the healer's compassionate imperatives?

Is this what I in youth did promise?
Is this what I, who thought the world
for you and me would be rhapsodic —
is this what I did, my once-beloved?

In what spheres is your mind now constrained?
What ghosts in me do your eyes see?
What anguish in your heart so filled with pain,
what does your soul now feel for me?

Why at the void are your eyes staring,
why from one vacant orb does a tear cling
denied even the moment's mating with another
which would produce heart's ease?

Why are thy lips so frigid
and thy poor heart a hardened seed?
Why is thy face so stern, so rigid,
thy once-fair hair like a dried weed?

Where is thy passion and thy flame,
thy laughter and thy maiden bliss?
Where is thy glance that will salve my shame?
Oh, why has a wraith as cruel as this
defaced you and led you lame
into this dreary plutonian crypt?

What now is the meaning of your living?
What now is the purpose of my seeing
you, my lost love, forever mired
in this advanced philanthropy,
where neither church nor friends extend
a helping hand despite our pleas,
where our society's feigned giving
proves naught but sheer hypocrisy?

Why has thy mind bolted its portals?
Why is thy stare a void gaze?
Why is this sickness for certain mortals
a reason to be buried in Minos' maze?

Isn't this interment for the deranged,
whose mates and healers condemned their wits
and decreed that all cursed with such odd stigmas
should be cast into these dreary pits?

Why do you stare as if the insane,
you think, should be out in the streets,
and those who claim a healthy brain
should be the ones inside these cells?

What is the meaning of your laughter,
the twitching of your forlorn face,
first your loathing, then your anger
against this hateful haven's state
where you are fed in meanest fashion
on food that's fit for lowly beasts?
You are robed in wretched fashion,
draped in rags which are not stitched.

Your recreation's but a circumscribed staring
at your rhythmic, beating, long-nailed feet
or at the odd-shaped, random ink stains,
which are psychiatrists' perverted wit.

And if thy lips are tempted to frame
the latent desires within your breast,
officialdom's stifling, swift reprisals
again debase your waning will,
forcing it into a sublimated prayer
as you relax, haltered like a beast.

Such stringent tyranny you'd never find
in my poor home, my poor abode,
for you well know my wretched kind
are proud cowards, who would revolt
against society's established forms.
Yet as a coward I joined the others
to fight our battle of Armageddon,
only to perish, to cease forlorn
in my rapacious, penal boredom.

For I did lure and did embrace
the concubines of officialdom
who mutilated your once-proud grace
inside these chambers of martyrdom.

And once embroiled in their plots,
dejected, desperate, and frenzied,
into existence's dank, unweeded garden
I stumbled. And I fell
exhausted against its jagged
and serpentine, granite wall.

Ah, what a feeling! My mind spun
when I perceived that mournful hall,
enveloped by hellish sneerings
and encircled by that omnipotent wall.

Fondly my heart maintained
that such a keep was made of gold.
Yet such a den and its society proved
to be the tarnished emblems of the world,
fair on their surface, but false in their depths.

And thus tormented with noble pity
for what I heard and what I upheld,
I asked myself, who are the guilty?
And then I cursed and spat upon
the day, the moment, that I was born.

For standing there on that ill-ridden,
cruel, and hellish abysmal brim
I heard my conscience crying, screaming
to the old, mythical Lernean beast
which now was choking my life's desire,
my once-young, proud, but fallen dream.

It seemed I saw the lethal, spewn venom
of that ferocious, nine-headed beast—
the fiendish mental Hydra—that ghoulish demon,
who fast paralyzed my cowering soul,
tore its flesh, crunched its bones,
until I cried, "Beast! Damned be your lord!
My dream is dead. I stand alone.
You have devoured it, it is no more,
bloodthirsty creature. No more. No more.
You sucked its life. Damn your creator
and all above."

Silence prevailed. I bowed and swayed,
but God's forgiveness I did not ask,
for in my hands I felt I held and waved
the slimy serpent which I had crushed.

But you, lost love, immune to horrors
except the ones that sucked your brains,
have stood by me asking no favors,
shedding no tears, feeling no pains,
convinced that all your mind's tremors
and all your heart's inhuman strains
into oblivion's uncharted plains
will come to rest, and then will fade.

                    Part II
This stark prelude, this dark beginning
had marked the day and the time
when I abandoned each human feeling.
I embraced the lethal tide
of a society that had no meaning,
no shame, no honor, and no pride.
All its forlorn, decrepit vassals

are hooded with stygian black,
and its chieftains are vile, banal,
and hollow as a rifted flask.

This society's purpose was subjugation
of each and every ethereal thought
by the abominable obliteration
of the body's defenses and those of the soul.

It is a society that is a merchant
dealer in death, an abortive fraud,
who in trading its wares, some new some old,
corrupts the young, neglects the old
who in their journey have lost their way
and stumble against life's jagged wall.

It is not that I beseech forgiveness —
either from you or from God —
for such infectious, dastardly ugliness
that I do labor to pen my wrath,
but to inure my being to punishment
until the day when I'll be judged.

For I am the lord of my brief life,
the secret affliction of my soul,
and as a lord, with regal pride,
alone, I'll stand, alone I'll fall.

And if society's corrupting morals
have touched my inner, tranquil thoughts,
it is because my soul's grand portals
unguarded stood, and I'm at fault.

And fall I will, and lone I'll suffer
exposing all the mire of soul
to every one now and hereafter,
until my agony becomes my world.

I'll architect my self-damnation
and to my hell I'll be my host.
For I embraced vile temptation,
my spirit I gambled and have lost.

I am my Lord's unique creation,
yet to my life I am the lord
and captain of my destination,
although my ship I'm steering wrong.

But though I'm bold and devil-ridden,
yet fearless as the god Poseidon,
I take no leave to implore the heavens
and ask for help from above.

Should I, with all my life's shortcomings,
add the audacity of a presumptuous request
and become blasphemous by so imploring
and importuning my one, true God?

Should I with all the sheer decadence
of once-rational mind and thought
that God bestowed upon my being
add hypocrisy as the last affront?

Never today, never tomorrow,
never in future, if future be,
such blasphemy will I allow
to kill my creed's divinity.

But stormy seas I'll plot and plow,
and tempest fearless I will seek,
and never, never will I allow
the present or the future to call me weak —
as long as in my veins and marrow
pure blood is running that is Greek.

No libations and no repentance
will ever alter my crooked path
since the proud arrogance of my existence
rejects the mercy of my true Lord.

For well I know at the first instance
of lust and sin, blindly I'll fall
without a drop of human resistance,
and my repentance I'll never uphold.

I need no sympathy, I need no pity,
my happiness I'll share with all;
but of my agony I am too chary,
I'll share my pain with none.

Part III

Stranger, behold this carnal frame,
perceive the nature of my soul,
and ask yourself, "Am I the same —
a traitor to men, a sinful thrall?
Or am I what my angered brother
has said he is and even more?"

Perceive the forceful, dismal tides
slowly eroding my human shore,
and as you read these dreary lines,
oh, stranger! pause and hear the roar
of my bleak soul pounding her marges
begging for everlasting liberty.

Hark! and listen with your mind
and heart's unerring, candid eyes.
Sample, and quaff this bitter brine
that is immolating my dark insides.

And then only will you realize
that I am you, and you are I,
and that my crimes are what you prize,
and that our souls never will be free.

But slaves today, and thralls tomorrow
they are, oh, stranger, and they will be,
since hoodwinked in darkness we followed
our "far-advanced" society
where neither candor nor simple justice
reigns and governs; but anarchy,
debased morals, and a fantastic,
human bloodthirsty satiety,
as our Tyrannos, rule our masses
with everlasting infamy.

Here the warped, the Ananias-like,
the twisted, and rapacious loves
are glorified in our minds
where vile desire negates established laws.

Ours is a society debased, polluted
with human greed, crime, and gore,
with foundations loosely constructed
by a decadent, inhuman pestilence
which tramples down the destitute,
corrupts the flesh, corrupts the soul,
and robs the meek who are ever forced
into oblivion before they are born.

For this society's high institutions,
its churches, its hospitals, and banks
are nothing but the poor's erosion —
a rich man's circus, his iron clutch
wherein the needy meet the extortions
of banker, doctor, and of priest.

These forms of human pestilence,
these bold, malevolent hypocrites,
are the mailed fist whose stranglehold
upon the throat of all beneath
paralyzes volition and all will
and burgeoning force and mobile desire
and drops, soulless, the societal corse,
enfeebled by its unholy ministrations
at its impious, destructive, brazen feet.

Part IV
My Lord, forgiveness I am not asking
though blasphemous I should not be,
but I detest those ugly lies
Your servants impose upon me.

For when I witnessed your lenient judgment
of those who err, oh Lord, my Lord,
amid my suffering I searched and found
that you are not as I had thought.

You never cared that I was bound
to oblivion's plains since I was born.
You never once made me feel proud
of all your teachings which I had loved.

So, why now should I remain
a bounden slave to your word
and not my life entertain
with what I gained as lore?

I've lived, I've sinned, and still am living
for I have conquered my nature's soul.
I'll live forever boldly upholding
my self-created inner world

because you abandoned me when I was born.

One day in future, distant times
these mystic, fragmentary thoughts
will subjugate man's dreary tides
and he will live fearing naught.

Let it be known that those who follow
must brave alone what I have braved,
and never bow their heads and pray
to an alien lord whom they cannot see.

This my centaurian perception
revealed to me, and I agree,
for I have found my soul's redemption
in my own thoughts, and not in thee.

For me, my Lord, you've ceased existing.
And if such thoughts are blasphemy,
advance, and prove that all my grievings
flowed not from thine own blasphemy
which you have thrown upon my life
with such ungodly infamy.

Part V

Mortal I am, my own Satrapes,
also the tyrant of my weak soul.
I ever condemn to the hungry harpies
this rotten flesh, thus to spare the worm.

And being an archon of my dark fate,
whose dirges are the hapless song,
the self-damnation, the lyric traits
of those who erred but stood alone;
now, in turn I'll face creation's

dark-veiled oblivion with that song
thus inured to all reproach
and immune to godly condemnation.

When the last flicker of life's pallid candle
is obscured by the darkness of Pluto's realm,
long Gea's hymen I'll pierce, and dive
into her dank, soft-lined womb
with all my flesh and striving mind,
and I will await my new birth once more.

For like a poem dithyrambic,
one future day I'll sprout forth
to praise rebirth in mode iambic
bearing my own judgment's sword.

For I have pierced God's feigned existence,
his life's and death's bacchanal theme
when I embraced my inward wisdom
after the catharsis of all my sins.